Picking Up The Broken Pieces

My Journey Through Psychosis, Depression and Anxiety

ARIELLE BRADBERRY

 FriesenPress

Suite 300 - 990 Fort St
Victoria, BC, V8V 3K2
Canada

www.friesenpress.com

Copyright © 2020 by Arielle Bradberry
First Edition — 2020

This memoir is written to the best knowledge of the author. The intention is to provide readers with an understanding of her mental health journey. The author does not have any medical credentials and therefore wants it to be known that all words written are of personal experience and opinion.

All rights reserved.

No part of this publication may be reproduced in any form, or by any means, electronic or mechanical, including photocopying, recording, or any information browsing, storage, or retrieval system, without permission in writing from FriesenPress.

ISBN
978-1-5255-7389-7 (Hardcover)
978-1-5255-7390-3 (Paperback)
978-1-5255-7391-0 (eBook)

1. BIOGRAPHY & AUTOBIOGRAPHY, PERSONAL MEMOIRS

Distributed to the trade by The Ingram Book Company

CONTENTS

Introduction	1
Chapter 1: Character/The Buildup	3
Chapter 2: Brain Crash	9
Chapter 3: Valentine's Hell	21
Chapter 4: A Little Less Psychotic	31
Chapter 5: Depression	35
Chapter 6: The Light at the End of the Tunnel	41
Chapter 7: Christmas Stress	51
Chapter 8: Déjà Vu	55
Chapter 9: My Journal	61
Chapter 10: Family Members' Perspectives	77
Chapter 11: Understanding Mental Illness	83
APPENDIX	89
My Tips to Help a Person Struggling with Mental Illness	*89*
Canadian Mental Health Association Tips for Supporting Someone You Love	*90*
Suggestions of Things to Bring to a Mental Health Facility	*91*
Phone Apps	*92*
Website with Mental Health Resources in Canada	*92*
Acknowledgments	93

INTRODUCTION

This is a memoir about my journey through psychosis, depression, and anxiety. I relive this traumatizing experience in my head every year right before Christmas time. As soon as the snow hits, so does the anxiety. I try everything to push past the feelings and cope, but they are still there. I have wanted to write about my experience post-recovery, but it has not been until January 2019 that I am sitting down and writing what happened to me in the year of 2015.

I will first discuss a little about myself and my family life, to give my readers a good understanding that mental health issues can occur at any time in one's life, and that it can truly happen to anyone. I believe there is a stigma attached to mental illness, and I hope by writing this novel I can break some of that stigma and portray to my audience the importance of taking care of yourself. I also hope to reach employers and encourage them to see the warning signs in their employees and not overwork them to the point of a mental breakdown. I will not be using any real names, locations, workplace names, job titles, the name of the hospital I was in to ensure this remains anonymous. I am strong and proud of what I have accomplished, and therefore I have decided to share my actual name.

CHAPTER 1

Character/The Buildup

I have the best family and extended family in the world. I'm not sure if I would have made it through my terrible experience without the love and support of each and every one of them. I grew up in a very small town with a loving mother, father, and three siblings. I have two older sisters and a younger brother, making me a middle child. I have lived a pretty simple and carefree childhood and teenage life. My parents have been married over thirty years. I have been very healthy, and have never been abused. There is no history of drug or alcohol abuse in my immediate family. I have tried weed a few times in high school and university and did not enjoy its effects; I have not tried any other drugs—I have never even tried a cigarette in my life. I drink occasionally, and the only time I drank more than a few was when I went to university. As many young adults do, I had fun and went to parties, but was not by any means a drug or alcohol addict.

I am a bubbly, outgoing, and humorous person, and I always have a smile on my face no matter how I feel. I also have a caring and sensitive, sympathetic personality like my mother. I enjoy playing soccer, ultimate frisbee, hiking, singing, and new adventures. I tend to be an over-thinker and can be very hard on myself. I rarely wear makeup as I am comfortable with who I am. The only time you will see me wearing makeup is for special occasions or times I just feel like looking better. I am a person who is comfortable in my own skin and I do not sugarcoat many things. If you want an honest opinion, I'm your person. I have always been way ahead of my age. I typically get along with people who are older than me because I am a forward-thinker and goal setter. Even as a child, I was constantly planning my life and wanting to be older than I was. This also makes me very stubborn and impatient.

I majored in psychology at university, but decided to graduate with a three-year bachelor of arts degree so I could go to college for human resource management. I found university extremely hard and I would freeze up every time I had to do a multiple-choice test. My stronger suit in university was in writing essays, and I feel that it is the only reason I was able to graduate university. I had to work extremely hard and go for help and tutoring almost every day, but eventually all the hard work paid off. I loved college and excelled because it was more hands on, the class sizes were smaller, and I had a future career in mind.

In 2014, I got engaged to my high school sweetheart and we were planning to get married in June 2015. I started dating my fiancé in grade twelve, but I have known him for most of my life. We went to public school together and our sisters are best friends. I am an extrovert and he is an introvert, and we bring out the best qualities in one another. We are both not confrontational people and because of this we rarely argue.

Our relationship has always been pretty easy because we are so perfect together. I am so lucky that I met my soul mate at such a young age.

My fiancé and I have been living in a two-bedroom apartment since 2013, which was shortly after we both graduated from school. We are the superintendents of our apartment building. We attended the same university except I had started one year before he did. He took an extra year in high school to ensure his grades were high enough to get into the kinesiology program. He graduated with a bachelor of science degree, then decided he wanted to work with his hands instead of perusing the academic route. My fiancé's father is a cabinet maker and had his own business for some time. My fiancé had grown up learning the skills of the trade, having worked with his father from a young age.

By 2014, I had worked for a medical company for two-and-a-half years. I knew my job very well and was able to assist other employees. I started to take on a larger workload. In addition to working as the front desk person, I took on the role of the human resources coordinator. I love new challenges and was always trying to impress my employers. I was a new graduate with a load of debt. I thought if I was a superstar at work I would quickly move up within the company and make more money. I took on as many work challenges that came my way, including terminating two employees and then working their jobs while trying to rehire new candidates and keeping up a busy medical clinic. I was successful in doing so, but mentally I was starting to dwindle.

In March 2014, my grandma passed away after battling dementia, and in December 2014, my grandpa passed away from cancer. This was an extremely sad time for my family. Much like myself, my mother was best friends with her mother and told her everything. It was so hard to see my mother so heartbroken and feel this terrible loss within our family. I loved my grandparents deeply, and took their deaths very hard.

The deaths of my grandparents, on top of planning for a wedding and trying to manage my new job responsibilities, became too much for me. I was no longer able to sleep at night; I lay in bed, thinking of all the things I had to complete, and I started to get paranoid during the nights my fiancé was working the night shift at work. I kept a knife beside my bed, thinking if there were any intruders, maybe I could fend them off. I was terrified by every single noise I would hear, even though we had lived in our apartment for many years. On my drives home from work, I kept having these thoughts that I was so good at my job and I was basically on top of the world. This led my brain to go into a weird power moment where I thought I could do anything, and I started to buy lottery tickets, thinking that I would win and become a millionaire. I also started thinking that I had ADHD because I could never sit still and was having a hard time focusing. At night, I would get home and sometimes just pace back and forth while my brain would be going a mile a minute, thinking about what I should do with my life and how I could make money so I could afford to start a family and buy a house.

There were so many warning signs, but I failed to see them because I was stuck in the bubble of wanting so many things in my life and being so stressed out. I kept saying to my fiancé that we needed to do something, that I must get out of this apartment. I suggested we book a hotel with a hot tub, and have a nice getaway for the night. My fiancé was currently battling a cold and did not want to go anywhere. Eventually, I convinced him that we should have something to look forward to, so we booked a hotel for Valentine's Day.

My body was slowly giving me signs of stress, too. I was having terrible stomach pains; in the mornings before I would go to work, I would gag and sometimes throw up, and have terrible diarrhea. I started to only be able to eat yogurt for breakfast, if that. Stomach pains weren't completely new for me though; I had started to have stomach pains in 2012.

I was told by my doctor that I had irritable bowel syndrome, and over the years I tried all sorts of stomach medications that never worked.

On January 11, 2015, I was suddenly awoken by a very loud banging on the door as if someone was trying to break into our apartment building. My fiancé had already left for work, so I got up to see what was going on. There was a woman at the door, saying her cousin had not shown up to work for two days and he had not replied to any of her text messages. She was afraid something terrible had happened to him, and insinuated he could be dead in his apartment. I took down her number and told her I would call the landlord to see if there was something we could do. This was a very strange encounter, and it left me terrified, wondering who was living in our building and what kind of trouble were they getting into to have their cousin thinking they could be dead. Fortunately, later that day the woman messaged me to say her cousin just had the flu really bad, and was not answering his messages. I had nightmares about the whole encounter.

CHAPTER 2

Brain Crash

The day my brain finally said "enough," I called my mom and told her that I was going to look into getting tested for ADHD. I was talking a mile a minute, explaining myself, but she didn't agree with me. I knew there was something wrong; I just didn't know what is was, or how I could fix it. I left the call feeling a bit angry and frustrated. I thought I would need her to help diagnose ADHD, as she knew me well and was my mother. I felt I needed something to explain my irrational behavior. After we ended the conversation, I headed to work.

At work, I stared at my computer screen, not knowing what to work on, it was as if I was frozen. I had a client come in and ask me a bunch of questions that I normally knew the answers to and I just stared at him blankly and said, "I'm sorry I can't think right now, I am stressed." The client said, "Don't worry about it, my wife is the same way when she gets stressed out." In the middle of the day, when our office closed during lunch, I just felt the urge to lie on the floor. I felt so exhausted; I lay there for a few minutes and just felt strange. I called my fiancé and told him that I was having an off day. We chatted for a little bit, and I felt better.

When I got home from work, I took a shower and all of a sudden, I started screaming, swearing, and repeating words over and over again. I felt as if I was in a trance. I knew the words were coming before I said them and that I had no control. I thought that my life was now going to be taken over by my brain, and I would continue throughout my whole life without actually knowing it was passing by. I got out of the shower, put on some clothes, and called 911. I had no idea what was happening to me. I stood on the driveway, waiting for the ambulance to come. So many weird thoughts were going through my head. I have never had such intense feelings and strange emotions before in my life. As I got into the ambulance, I was trying to answer the questions of the paramedics while I was thinking, *this is all part of my life; this is supposed to be happening right now.*

When I got to the hospital, I fell to the ground and was acting as if I was a child. I kept saying, "I remember my whole past life." I was taken to a room and tested twice for drugs, and everything came back clean both times. I then went into a different room where I started swearing and laughing. I thought that I had multiple personality disorder, and everyone that has ever met me was in the hospital because they were all part of this "study" that was about my life and my unique case. I could hear voices of high school friends, past boyfriends, family friends, and employers. I distinctly remember hearing a childhood friend named Amber just swearing and laughing, saying "the time has fucking come, you are now going to be famous." I remember giving the front desk my phone and information to contact my family, my benefits card, but from there most of the night is a blur.

The next thing I do remember was one of the psychiatrists grabbing me and taking me to a room and pushing me onto a chair and I bumped my head against the wall. I was so upset and as he left the room, I stuck my foot out to trip him. This is very out of character for me as I would normally never do something like that. I was then sent to the bottom floor to a room called "peekaboo"—this is not the real name of course, but it was something similar. This room had a mattress on the floor and a metal toilet, and it resembled jail. I was so tired I just passed out on the mattress. When I awoke, I thought I was in jail for drinking and driving and killing someone. I used to drive a white Neon when I was about eighteen years old. There was a hit-and-run that happened in a town about twenty minutes from my parents' place. Whenever I visited my parents, I would see this sign posted with a white Neon, stating that they are trying to find the person who killed someone in a hit-and-run while driving a white Neon. It of course was not me, but I thought that must be why I was in jail. I was signed in on a form three, meaning I was under the category of involuntary admission, and I was not allowed to leave.

I was so confused. My parents were there, and they were upset. I asked them for some paper and began writing down all my thoughts. This is what it looked like, spelling errors included. All names have been changed except ones that don't have any relation or meaning.

ARIELLE BRADBERRY

Tammy	Joe	Trudy
Tina	Bob	Bodie
Teddy Bear	Cynthia	Yashi
John	Mia	Zaro
Serena	James	Sporty
Tim	Thomas	Timid
No No No	Arthur	Fat
Upset stomach	Ethan	Skinny
Paranoid Schitzophreni		Personalities

Dec 12	-abused	Baby
want a cigarette as a 9 year old	-rape	Child
abuse	-car accident	Adult
Aunt Tina? I want a new Aunt?	-Different person	female
2	-Wheel Char	male
I want to punch something	-glasses	funny
Serena Jillian Clark	-perfessional	
Tammy Clark John Clark	-empathetic	
	-OCD	
	-ADHD	

Multiple personalities 1 more to go

PICKING UP THE BROKEN PIECES

Dad is John and he drove Tammy and I home in when Tammy didn't want to but did anyways, she was pregnant with me while Susie gave birth and we got swapped at birth. I lived, but Julie didn't so I have been feeling survival guilt. That is why I get along with Julie which is me.

My dad died on my 12th birthday

06-12-2005

The 12th of each month I have an issue that was yesterday

I Thought he died, but he went to jail & is now back for my 25th birthday and wants to see me get married. John is my dad he is married to Tammy.

I tried to figure out what had happened to me. Many different scenarios came into my head. A lot of the visions came from shows I was watching or books that I had read. The one about the birthday clearly came from the movie *Fifty First Dates*. The nurses would come in and ask my age or what year it was and I would give them a different answer each time. As you can see on the previous page, I thought I was born in 2005, which would have made me a five-year-old. Also, my family members' names I had written down are not their names, and not just for the sake of this story, but I actually said my dad was John, which is not true.

My mom told me while they were waiting for me to wake up, the nurses and staff kept directing them to the pamphlets on drug addictions and my parents said to them, "We know our daughter does not do drugs." One nurse said to my parents, "Yeah, that's what all the parents think until they find out their children are on drugs." I do not do drugs, and I had absolutely no drugs in my system. The psychiatrist told them they believed I was going through acute psychosis, or I may be bipolar. This was a very confusing and frustrating time for myself and my whole family.

Eventually I was moved to the psychiatric ward, into a room in that I shared with an individual who had bipolar. I was given a tray of food for breakfast. It was a typical hospital tray with a divider down the middle. I was given coffee, juice, a muffin, a fruit cup, and cereal. All I could remember thinking is that I was being studied based on what I eat, side A or side B. I was trying to choose who I was and what I would like to eat.

After a few days, I had a CT scan done to make sure there was nothing wrong with my brain, and everything came back clear. Then I had a psychologist evaluate me, and she determined that I was going through acute psychosis brought on by stress. The definition of psychosis from the Canadian Mental Health Association website states, "Psychosis is a serious but treatable medical condition that reflects a disturbance in brain functioning. A person with psychosis experiences some loss of contact with reality, characterized by changes in their way of thinking, believing, perceiving and/or behaving. For the person experiencing psychosis, the condition can be very disorienting and distressing. Without effective treatment, psychosis can overwhelm the lives of individuals and families." *(https://cmha.ca/understanding-mental-illness/psychosis, 2020 CMHA National)*

My family came and visited me every day. Sometimes I didn't believe my family members were actually my family. Some days I would say I was someone else, or that my whole family was dead. Other days I said I was a child, or pregnant. I also said to my very thin sister, "Wow you look great; you used to be really fat." My sister has never been overweight, so I am not sure where that thought process came from, but she laughed about it. That must have been so bizarre for my family to experience. I spoke as though I knew what was going on, but I was not making much sense at all. They found humour in the things that I said, but this also made the whole experience unnerving.

Throughout the time in the hospital I distinctly remember always staring in the mirror and thinking I looked different than I remember. I would look in the mirror and think, *who am I*. I was so confused and constantly having different scenarios run through my head. I had so many flashbacks to my childhood. There was a picture that came to mind in particular of me and a girl that I had to gone to public school with for a brief period. This picture stuck out in my head because when I looked in the mirror one day, I thought I looked just like the friend in the picture, and then thought that I had a twin. I constantly was confused by who I really was and would sometimes say I was Black, even though I am Caucasian.

There was a common room in the psych area of the hospital where we would go to eat and play games, and there was a piano. One day, I sat on the piano bench, playing away, thinking that I was amazing and that I was playing the most beautiful melodies. In reality I was horrible, and some of the other patients were yelling at me to stop playing. There was one lady who had told me I was good at playing the piano, so this made me think that I was a professional pianist. I also would sing while playing the piano, which likely sounded even worse than what I was playing, which certainly did not match what I was singing.

I met so many unique individuals in the hospital with a variety of different mental health issues. One man in particular was an amazing artist who was a drug addict and suffered from depression. This man was unbathed, had wild hair, but was so sweet. One day I thought the reason I was in the hospital was because I was supposed to help all the patients feel better. I went up to the man and said, "I think it would be good for you if you took a shower and went and got yourself a haircut, it will make you feel so much better." He had told me he was feeling really down and that's why he hadn't showered. I hugged him and said, "feel better," and then he told me he was thinking of getting a mullet just like he had back when he was a teenager. I said if he wanted that haircut he should go for it. A couple days later, I walked past the man who was now showered and he said, "Hey, check out my new haircut." He had taken my advice and gotten a mullet with lines shaved on the sides as part of a design. He seemed happier, and I felt I was doing a good job.

There was this one man in the hospital who freaked me out, and he would say inappropriate things. I was at a group therapy class and this guy came in and was saying inappropriate things, but not directed toward me. I ran back to my room, having weird flashbacks. This flashback in particular was from a university party. The flashback was about a party my roommates were having. I had just come downstairs after having had a shower, and was heading out to go meet a friend. This guy that I had met before came up to me and said, "You look sexy with your hair wet." This was a super awkward encounter, but anyway, that was it. I left and met my friend. While I was crying into my pillow at the hospital, I kept hearing "you look sexy with your hair wet." All of a sudden, I thought I knew what had happened to me: I had been raped. I did not remember the name of this guy, but I kept saying different names in my head and trying to figure it out.

The person that was in charge of the group therapy session had gotten my psychiatrist. When my psychiatrist came into my room, I told him that I was upset because I remembered being raped. After my psychiatrist left, I grabbed the fuzzy blanket my parents had brought to the hospital for me. The blanket was comforting, and as I held it tight to my face, I could smell fresh linen. The smell was so strong and not actually how my blanket smelled, but it was like my brain could make different smells occur that I felt were real.

We later had a family meeting, and I was told I could call my old roommate and find out if she remembered much from that night. To be clear, I was never raped and nothing bad had happened to me that night, but due to the psychosis I was not in a clear mindset and I kept thinking of events that hadn't actually occurred. I am so embarrassed to this day, knowing that I called my old roommate and had asked her questions. I can't imagine what my parents were thinking at the moment as well. No one in my family really knew what psychosis was. I had learned about it in school, but didn't remember what it was.

Another moment in the hospital that is even more embarrassing to talk about is when I thought that I was a teenager again and I was in the hospital with my former boyfriend from grade nine. There was a patient who had curly hair just like him, but looked absolutely nothing like him, and I thought we had both been in some sort of accident and that we were in the hospital together. One night I left my room and crawled into the bed beside him and gave him a kiss and said, "Soon this will be all over and we will be back together." He had awful smoke breath. I had no idea what was going on, but I heard someone coming and I quickly ran out of the room, leaving my slippers behind. There were males and females on the same floor of the hospital, but not in the same rooms. The nurses did their rounds and checked the rooms at night, but the fact that I ventured into a male's room and did this horrifies me. In my opinion, there should be separate floors for males and females. All I could think about when I was recovered from the psychosis is what if he had tried to have sex with me, anything could have happened. Thank goodness I left the room and nothing more had happened. It wasn't until my antipsychotic medication started to work that I started to realize that my fiancé was indeed my fiancé and I broke down crying, telling him what I had done. My fiancé said, "It's okay, you were not well and you were very confused. I forgive you."

After a few weeks in the hospital I was allowed to leave for a few hours and take trips with my family. One night my parents came and took me out for dinner with my whole family and my fiancé. While I was at the restaurant, my mom kept asking if I was okay and I guess because she was asking this, I thought there must be something really wrong with me. All of a sudden

I thought that I was like the girl in the novel *The Fault in Our Stars* and that I couldn't see that I had an oxygen tank, but that it was there and that I was sick. When we were leaving the restaurant, I started walking slowly and acting as if I was that girl. After being in the hospital for a few weeks, I was finally signed off to go home, but I was by all means not better. I was on antipsychotic medication, and sleeping pills for nighttime. I had no idea what was going on with me and I took whatever the doctors gave me. I had become reliant on the sleeping pills that I had never before taken in my life.

CHAPTER 3

Valentine's Hell

When I was discharged, I went back home with my fiancé. He was working at the time and I was to stay home. I filled my days with watching TV, playing on my keyboard, dancing, and lip synching. I would play on my keyboard and record my playing. I thought that I was playing "Für Elise" by Beethoven and other famous songs without even having to read any music. My fingers were just going crazy on the keyboard, and I thought my hands were almost magical.

I was clearly still going through psychosis, and one memory that sticks out is my mind is a delusion I had. My fiancé is a huge basketball fan, and he got a basketball game that he would play on his PlayStation that was connected to the internet. In this game, he had to put some general information about himself and choose answers to what he would do in an interview, the type of player he is, his height, etc. I often watched him play this game. Suddenly, I heard a helicopter on the roof of our building, and while my fiancé was playing, I packed him a bag with all his basketball stuff and then went and convinced him we needed to go outside. I thought that there was someone who was coming to pick him up and draft him for the NBA because this was their new way of picking players. I thought that they used video game to get into the minds of basketball players and then they would draft them and train them. My fiancé was such a great person through all this, and he went outside with me. Of course, there was no helicopter, and I snapped out of the situation a bit and told him about my thoughts.

Valentine's Day was quickly approaching, and my fiancé said he thought it was not a good idea to go to the hotel that we had booked for Valentine's night. I of course protested greatly, I cried and convinced him that I really needed a night out. He said as long as I was feeling much better by that date we would go.

After a few weeks of being home, I stopped having so many psychotic thoughts and I was starting to seem more normal mentally. I still was feeling strange; the sun seemed extra bright and I felt sick and drained. I realize now this was part of the side effects of the antipsychotics. My father's boss's wife experiences issues in the winter, and she recommended a natural supplement that helped align her brain. My parents purchased this natural remedy for me and suggested this could help with how I was feeling. At the time, no one knew that this was a terrible idea and I should have been following what my psychiatrist recommended only. My parents tend to go for natural remedies rather than what doctors recommend. This is mainly because they witnessed what all the medication my grandma was on and their side effects did to her.

On Valentine's Day, we packed our bags and headed to the hotel. I took one of the natural pills my parents had given me. Shortly after we checked in, I decided I wanted to take a shower. As I was having a shower, I had so many weird thoughts going through my head, for example, I thought I was meant to be a baby maker. I thought that once we tried for a baby, the baby would form in about two days instead of the typical forty weeks. I thought I was this special person that would be a surrogate for all the people I knew that couldn't have babies.

After we had enjoyed some time in the hot tub, we went to the hotel's restaurant for dinner. It was so nice, and I relaxed and decided to have a beer. My mind just kept thinking all sorts of strange things. I thought that there was another room in the backside of the restaurant that was more of a club and all of my bridesmaids and close girlfriends were back there waiting to surprise me with a bachelorette party. I actually texted one of my friends and asked if they were at the hotel I was at. I was trying to see if she would give it away somehow. She was likely very confused.

After dinner, I started acting very weird and my fiancé decided we should check out of the hotel right away and go home, as he was worried something bad was going to happen. As we stood at the desk, I started to sing "O Canada" quietly, and eventually I was singing at the top of my lungs. Then I thought my friend from another province had come in on a helicopter to surprise me for this bachelorette party. I started running around the hotel, yelling her name and looking for her. I remember hearing her in my head calling me back, and I thought that if I took off my clothes, I would be able to run faster. I threw off my purse and shirt and was running around the lobby. Eventually I was grabbed by the police and taken into a separate room. The police handcuffed me and was asking my fiancé questions. My fiancé answered their questions and let them know that I was going through psychosis. Eventually the paramedics arrived and I remember yelling at one of the paramedics to sing and that I knew he was a good singer. The paramedic broke out and sang "Ave Maria" and he was really good. This actually did happen—my fiancé has confirmed this is true, and not just a delusion I had. The paramedics gave me a tranquilizer in the leg to calm me down. The needle hurt so bad. I was strapped to a board and was not able to move at all. This is the most horrific part of my whole journey. I absolutely hate it when I can't move; I won't even sleep in a sleeping bag. I was taken back to the hospital and readmitted.

I was put into an overnight area with rooms that had doors that were clear and locked. This was not in the psych ward, but a waiting type area where I would stay until there was room on the psych ward. I kept singing "O Canada" while in this overnight waiting area, in different voices and with different accents. I had more delusions happening during this time, it was as if the psychosis was worse now. I thought that I was the guy from the *Lord of the Rings* and that I had a precious ring, which in this case was my engagement ring. I slid my ring along the floor and whistled like a bird saying, "Here pretty pretty, I have your precious. Want a cracker?" I kept calling to the person in the office who was watching the rooms and talking like a parrot. I said "my precious" to my engagement ring multiple times. I caught the attention of the nurse and rolled my ring across the floor. The nurse got my ring and told me to keep it on my finger. Thank goodness, I did not lose my engagement ring. When my fiancé came to visit me he took it with him so that I would not lose it.

I had to use the washroom so I kept calling for someone to let me out, but no one would come. The door may not have been locked, but from what I remember is I could not get out. I remember peeing in the corner with my clothes on. Eventually someone did come in and I got a new pair of pants and had to go commando. The lack of staff and poor treatment within this hospital was horrifying.

Another terribly embarrassing thing that I did was go to the bathroom, take a shit, and put it into my pants and see how long I could walk with it in there until it fell out. I thought I was in a weird competition on TV and that if I won, I would get a prize. I must have been thinking of an episode from the show "The League" where they do all sorts of weird competitions to choose who gets to draft first in their fantasy football league. There was one episode in particular where one of the character's kids was taking their poo out of the toilet. This of course is super disgusting and awkward to talk about it, but I told my friend Amber that I would include this because I called her a few days later and told her about it. Amber knows I am writing this book, and she wanted me to include this story of when I called her on the phone while I was in the hospital. I had called her, talking completely normal, and said, "Hey Amber, I'm in the hospital I am being treated so poorly. Today the people were so mean that I took a shit and smeared it all over the floor." I told her all sorts of stories as if I was totally okay, but I was obviously not making any sense at all. I also told her that there was a baby that was flushed down a pipe and ended up in China and that the people who found the baby are now taking care of it as their own. Amber remembers me talking so normally, but the words that were coming out of my mouth were so bizarre. She told me that after that event she stopped smoking weed because she was afraid something like this may happen to her.

Amber has come in and out my life many times. Our parents are best friends, so I get to see her every Christmas Eve, but other than that, we don't see each other as much as we did when we were kids growing up together. Amber is a beautiful, confident woman who was very popular throughout school and has many friends. She actually went through a great number of mental health issues prior to my psychosis that I had no understanding of. My mom would tell me about some of the major depression and anxiety that Amber was going through, and I thought something terrible must have happened to her during college to explain why she was going through depression. I was one those people at the time who had so many misconceptions about mental illness, and I did not have a clue about the suffering and pain it brought. I have since learned that mental illness can come at any time in one's life, and it does not mean that you came from a bad family, did drugs, or had a traumatic experience. It doesn't matter if your life is perfect or not, you can still experience mental illness.

One of the weirdest delusions I had was that I was a Russian spy, and that I had to train in my room to eventually break out and join my family at the "safe" airplane. I thought that I needed to talk to people and write down all the names of the people I liked in the hospital. My dad is an electrician, and I thought that over the years he has been working as an electrician he was actually setting up bombs. My job was to tell my dad who all the people good were so that he could make sure to have them come into the airplane so we would all be in it when he blew up Canada.

My parents came to the hospital as soon as they had found out that I had been readmitted. One the nurses said to my mother, "Just face it, your daughter is bipolar." My mother is the type of person who never speaks up to other people and avoids confrontation like the plague, just like me. My mom turned to that nurse and said, "Hey, I am also a nurse and I'm positive that you cannot make any type of diagnosis nor should you be making assumptions. She was here a few weeks prior for psychosis, and it is clear that she has been under a ton of stress, and that is why she is mentally ill." I think my mother-in-law, who was with her, was never so proud of my mom. My mother-in-law is the opposite of my mom, and I am surprised that she didn't punch that nurse in the face.

In the hospital this time around, I met the nicest girl, and we would talk to frequently. I didn't know why she was in the hospital, but I assumed depression, because she had cuts all the way up her arms. She didn't know why I was in the hospital, either. In a way, the hospital was much like jail in the fact that you didn't talk about what you were in for, so to say. Almost every day I would see this girl looming winter hats. She said she was really into making hats, and she would make me one If I gave her some yarn. When I got a weekend pass, I picked out some yarn so she could make me one. I think it only took her about a day to make the hat, and it was so nice and warm.

While I was in the hospital, the doctors thought that I should have an EKG done to see what was going on with my brain. Part of the process was that I would have to stay up all night without sleep in order to do the test. I needed to sleep during the test so they could see sleep brain waves. I told the girl who makes the hats what I had to do, and she said she would stay up to keep me occupied. She and I walked around the wing and stopped in the hallway with a window. We started blowing against the window at the same time so we could draw on it. This brought back childhood memories of doing this as a kid, and we turned to one another and laughed.

After a few weeks, the mood stabilizers I was taking started working much better and I again was able to go home. My parents felt it would be best if I went home with them and my mom would take time off work to monitor me. My fiancé would go to work and come to my parents' place on the weekends to see me. My parents live about an hour away so it wouldn't be bad, although my mom would have to drive to take me to my psychiatrist appointments and to the hospital if anything else came up.

The car ride to my first psychiatrist appointment was very interesting. I had chosen a music track on the 8 track, and was listening while lip-synching away. All of a sudden, I thought that I was famous, like Jimmy Fallon. I thought there was a paparazzi crew following my car and videoing me. I thought they had the same music on as me so they could hear the words and see me lip-synching. I got very into this role. We stopped at Tim Hortons and I put my sunglasses on and walked and acted like I was a famous person being followed. I also started to think that Jimmy Fallon was secretly my brother, but only I had figured it out. I thought that we both were very funny and that he soon was going to come and tell me himself that we were related.

On February 21, 2015, I had a wedding to attend at a very prestigious place. My parents agreed to drive me and Amber there, and my fiancé would meet us there. He would stay longer while I went back home with my parents. We went to the wedding, and I was unable to drink because of the medication I was on and of course it just would not be a good idea. I don't think anyone would have known I was not drinking because I had all sorts of strange conversations with friends. No one there had a clue that I was still going through psychosis, although very mildly as compared to before. I had a great time reminiscing with Amber and telling her all about how I was going to become famous one day.

CHAPTER 4

A Little Less Psychotic

I slowly started to become less psychotic and more lethargic. While I was recovering from the psychosis, I started to get extremely tired, full of laughter at random times, and having weird leg pains that would cause me to fall over sometimes. Also, a few times in the night I would wake up and not be able to move my body; it was as if I was paralyzed. I was now seeing my psychiatrist at his office once a week so I could be monitored and to see if I needed any medication adjustments. My psychiatrist thought maybe I had narcolepsy, which is a sleep disorder that can cause some of the symptoms that I had just described. He set me up to go to a sleep clinic so they could do some testing. The clinic was busy, so my appointment would be in a few weeks' time.

Since I had set up an appointment to go to the sleep clinic, I got a notice in the mail stating that they were taking away my driver's licence because I could be a risk on the road due to my extreme fatigue. I knew this was a possibility already, as my psychiatrist had said so, but it still felt weird knowing I would not being able to drive anywhere. Every day I felt worse, and by the time it came closer to my sleep appointment I ended up cancelling because I was feeling so awful and depressed.

My mom was working at a gym where she met an iridologist with whom she was talking to about me being so tired. This woman had a son who was always tired and she had taken him to a doctor, but she was never given an answer to why he was always so tired. She explained to my mom that she started to study iridology and started giving her son natural vitamins that helped him immensely. My mom thought I should check it out, so we went to this woman to get tested. She looked into my eyes and determined that I was experiencing adrenal fatigue. She had me close my eyes while I was standing, and she would hand different supplements to me and see how my body reacted to them to determine what would help the most. I got some of her supplements to try, but this was clearly not what was going on with me, and it did not help.

After time, I stopped having psychotic thoughts and was starting to feel a bit more normal so I felt it was time to go back to work. I returned to work, still feeling tired, but managing. I returned on a Wednesday and found they had hired another girl since I had been away for some time. I mostly helped out where I could. The following week I felt worse and asked my company if I could ease back into the job more and work part-time. They said that would not work so I tried my best to work full-time. After a few days, I had to call in sick because I couldn't eat at all and was throwing up constantly; I felt awful.

I was on and off at work because I clearly was not ready to return and felt an extreme drop in my mood. One day I talked to my boss about how I felt almost depressed and it was if I couldn't really enjoy things very much. We had a great conversation and she had talked about how she sometimes goes on an antidepressant, like Prozac. I wasn't feeling as if I was quite there yet, not knowing what was going on with my mood. A few days later as I was going to go to work in the morning, I felt like the world had come crashing down. I felt extremely depressed and I started crying for no reason. I just felt terrible and didn't feel like myself at all. I called a girl from work because my boss's phone was not working and I told her that I was feeling extremely low. I told her I would have to go on a leave of absence, but would keep in contact.

Every day I was at home I felt worse. I could no longer find humour in anything, not even the show *Modern Family*, which normally makes me laugh. It felt as all of the life had been sucked out of me and I could no longer feel anything. I would try and cry out the pain, but this gave me no relief. I started to question what the point of life was, and felt like I no longer wanted to live.

CHAPTER 5

Depression

After a few weeks off work I stopped throwing up and was feeling better physically, but mentally not one bit. The first weekend I was feeling less sick, we had a family get together at my parents' house. I was outside playing Frisbee with my siblings and fiancé when my mom said that some mail had come for me from my workplace. I still got mail from time to time from when I lived with my parents, and my boss knew I was staying with my parents, so I figured they might have sent me a card or something. I opened the letter from work and read that my company could no longer employ me because I had been off work too much. This was the most devastating news, especially at this time. I wanted to go back to work when I recovered. I missed all the patients that came in and chatted with me, and the employees with whom I had become close.

I couldn't imagine not being able to return to work when I was feeling better. The job loss made me feel like there was no hope left. We were already going into debt because we were living off one income and my fiancé had to take a lot of time off in order to stay with me. Now I would have to find a new job and I was no longer going to be receiving unemployment insurance or benefits.

The first thought of suicide popped into my head that day. I thought maybe I could find a rope in my parents' basement and hang myself on the tree that my friends and I used to build tree forts in. I got more depressed every day, and thoughts of suicide popped into my head often. Eventually I told my family how low I felt, and said if I was to kill myself would they forgive me. My fiancé said he would never forgive me, that it would be devastating. My family decided that I should go back to the mental health hospital to be checked in so I wouldn't do anything to harm myself.

I did not want to go back to that horrible place, but at the same time, I wanted to get better, and any hope of getting better would be good. I knew I would at least get to talk to my psychiatrist every day and see what they could do to help me get better. I got to the hospital to check in, and found out that since I no longer had benefits, I would be sharing a room with five other women. I knew it would be difficult to sleep, as the beds were all so close to one another. It literally felt as if I was in prison. I was not allowed to have my phone and because I was now going through depression, they had to take the strings off all my clothes for fear I may try to strangle myself.

I settled back into the hospital and was experiencing insomnia. My fiancé would come during the day when he was on nights, and come at night when he was on day shift. I had a few visitors each night, which made things a bit more tolerable. Throughout my hospital stay I tried to go to the group therapy sessions in order to pass some of the time, and I was hoping to see some sort of improvement. For some of the sessions we would rate our mood and I felt like zero was always the way I was feeling. I tried to go to the yoga class once a week, as it seemed like something that could be good for me, but my mood was at an ultimate low and I did not see the positives.

It was hard to sleep in a hospital room with five other women, especially since I am a light sleeper. I had major insomnia and was taking sleeping pills to help me sleep at night, but they would usually wear off around 2:00 a.m. I had a roommate who would start praying out loud at 5:00 a.m. and it would drive me crazy. I eventually was given a second sleeping pill that would help me sleep from 2:00 a.m. on. In the mornings I would lie in bed for as long as possible and I would eventually get up around 10:00 a.m. or later, missing breakfast but hoping that my day would feel less long.

I made a goal that no matter what, I would shower every day. Every morning when I finally rolled out of bed I would go for my shower and then eat a muffin or something that my mom had brought that I had stored in my drawer. Living felt impossible for me, and I just wanted the day to be over so I could go to bed. I started to take Prozac as an antidepressant, and was told it could take up to seven weeks for it to work. This seemed extremely unbearable, and the suicidal thoughts started to pop into my head more and more.

There was a vase of flowers in our room, and I thought maybe I could smash it and use the glass to slit my wrists. Of course, being in the psych ward, the vase was definitely plastic. When my family came to visit during the days, we would usually try to get outside for a walk or play cards. Playing games helped pass some time for me and I started to bring my own card games to the common room to see if other people wanted to play. The card games Wizard and Monopoly Deal were my favourites at the time, and it was easy to teach others to play as well.

After some time of the taking Prozac, I totally lost my appetite and would throw up after every meal. The medication was not helping at all and my mood was worse because I couldn't even keep any food down. Contrary to my first stay at the hospital, I now noticed how gross the food was. One of the weirdest breakfasts I had was a pancake sandwich with cheese and ham inside.

We would go to get our food in the common room and we would all eat there, or sometimes I would bring my food back to my room. My mom brought me home cooked meals and we would get a pass to go upstairs so I could reheat them. I would eat the meal my mom brought, and soon after run to the bathroom and throw up. I was able to keep down protein shakes sometimes, so I started drinking them more often. I stopped eating solid food because even the thought of eating would make me gag. Eventually I spoke with my psychiatrist to see if there was something else I could go on instead of Prozac, as I lost about fifteen pounds, which was a lot for me because I only weighed about 120 pounds. I was nervous that if I switched to Citalapram I would have to wait another seven weeks to see any results, but was informed that it would still count toward the time I had already waited, as it would slowly start to get into my system.

I would get on my phone and search blogs of other people going through depression to see if the antidepressants worked any sooner for them than what they had been told. I kept trying to find some sort of hope or happy ending. I read one blog in particular where the person wrote about wanting to jump in front of a car. That image stuck in my head and I debated doing the same thing when went for walks with my mom when she visited me in the hospital. I realize now that you have to be careful what you read when you are feeling depressed because it can make you feel worse. I realized the blogs I read were from years ago, and if I wanted to write a comment, I knew no one would reply because the blog was so old. When you're feeling depressed, the internet can be extremely frustrating because you never find the answers you are looking for, and you can actually feel more alone. I am not religious, but I found myself praying to God that I would feel better soon, and not be so depressed.

I had so many urges to hurt myself, just to feel something. I would lie in bed and sometimes try to smother myself with my pillow. I would pinch myself, or squeeze my head or throat tightly. I started to get a much better understanding of why people cut themselves. I had to say to myself over and over that this is not permanent; things will change; don't do anything you will regret later. I knew I did not want cuts on my wrists, and so I fought hard against my urges to hurt myself and would rather do things like pinch myself. If you have never been through extreme depression you might not understand, and probably think what I did was silly. Prior to my experiences, I thought people who cut wanted attention or did it because they hated their life. There are many reasons why people choose to cut their wrists, but I can say I understand the urge when you just want to feel something. Everyone has different experiences and you cannot fully understand how anyone else feels, but all I can say to people with this urge is stay strong and find something to get your mind off your bad thoughts other than self-harm.

My family started asking if we should consider postponing the wedding until I was feeling better. The thought of having to tell people we were changing the, date was terrifying especially because no one knew what I was going through and I felt they would think we were having relationship problems. I did not want anyone thinking that our relationship was flawed in any way, especially because I felt, and still feel that we are perfect for each other. I expressed to my family that the wedding was the only thing that I had to look forward to especially because now I didn't even have a job to go back to. I felt as though I literally had nothing keeping me going besides my family loving and supporting me. The wedding was still a month away, and I was hoping the anti-depressants would soon kick in. We realized that we would no longer be able to go to Jamaica for our honeymoon as planned; we would need to cut costs where we could, and it would not be wise to be in another country when needing to take medication and we wanted to have support close by if needed. Part of our new honeymoon plan was to go white water rafting and camp out for the night there, as staying in the cabin is also very costly.

One of the days my sister-in-law came to visit she suggested that I keep a journal where I write about anything positive, even if it is something small. The first thing I had written in my journal was that I felt a bit of hope when one of the social workers had said things must always get better once you have hit rock bottom. The only way is to go up. I felt that I knew things would eventually get better, and thought about my wedding day.

CHAPTER 6

The Light at the End of the Tunnel

After a few weeks of being in the hospital I felt like it was time to go home as I did not feel that I was progressing there anymore. My mom suggested I go to their house, and she would take time off work to stay with me. I checked out of the hospital and went to stay with my parents, where I could go for walks with my mom each day and eat better food. I also had a wedding to think about and start to plan a bit more.

Every day was really tough, and I knew my mom would not allow me to lie in bed all day like I had been doing in the hospital. We went for walks every day, and kept really busy. My mom went to a group therapy session with me one day to see if it would help to talk with other people. The group therapy session was in a dark, musty basement, and everyone was much older than I was. I felt like I got absolutely nothing out of the session and did not go back. This was a free group therapy, but I could not believe that it was held in the most depressing place. How can you call this therapy? I felt as though I was on a TV show in a very unpleasant AA meeting.

I kept plugging along, hoping I would soon feel better and every day wishing it was nighttime so I could go to sleep and another day would pass by. I was just hoping the medication would soon kick in and I wouldn't feel like ending my life anymore. One day something funny happened at the dinner table, and I smiled for the first time in forever. My mom noticed right away and said, "hey, you smiled! Maybe the medication is starting to kick in." After this moment, everyday got a little better, bit by bit.

I started to prepare for our wedding, and before I knew it the day arrived. On our wedding day, I smiled a lot and felt mostly happy. I only had two drinks to make sure that I didn't get worse as I was still on medication. We went white water rafting for our honeymoon and had a great time. I still was not feeling quite myself and I knew I would have enjoyed it much more before I became mentally ill. One day I would like to go white water rafting again, during a more pleasant time. I would also like to travel to Jamaica and have the honeymoon we both dreamed of.

My next life goal was to get off all my medications and work at moving on with my life. I tried to go cold turkey with Olanzapine, but I found myself reverting to how I felt before and throwing up constantly. I just wanted to feel like myself again. I ended up using a pill cutter and slowly cutting a bit off every few days. Weening myself off the medication was extremely hard, and I experienced many side effects. It took a long time, but I was finally off all medications and was still feeling great. I would never suggest doing this on your own. A psychiatrist should be the person who directs you to go off your medications.

I had to work through an agency in order to find a job, and it was difficult trying to think of an explanation for why I was off work for a year. I am a terrible liar, and told them I got a bad case of mono and was off sick for a long time and then lost my job due to my sickness. I was too worried to talk to any workplace about my experience for fear I would seem unreliable.

I finally found a job that was suitable and didn't cause me any anxiety. I worked with a human resources information system where I was to enter and update employee data for all the workers of the company. It was crucial that all the data I entered into the database was entered with precision. I am a detail oriented person. I triple-checked everything I entered and stared at my screen intently, making sure that no errors were made. After about six months, I was offered a contract. I felt so fortunate and happy that I had finally found the right job for me and I would also be receiving a better wage.

My husband and I desperately wanted to start a family, and figured if I got pregnant right away, I would be able to get maternity leave and hopefully I would get to return to my job. We had a son on November 1, 2017. Everything in my life seemed wonderful; I was so happy to finally be a mom.

The first few weeks of motherhood were extremely difficult. My son had a set of lungs that you would not believe. We had a hard time with sleep and I had a great deal of anxiety. I always heard from other people to sleep when the baby sleeps. I could not sleep. I was so worried my son would die of SIDS in his sleep. When I did fall asleep at night, I would wake in a panic, holding my pillow and thinking I was smothering my baby. After a few weeks of getting little to no sleep, I started to feel as if I didn't really need any sleep. I was full of energy, but really stressing about the fact that my husband was going back to work and I would have to take care of our son by myself. I would work hard at being a great stay-at-home mom and wife.

A few days before my husband was to return to work, I went into a trance-like state early in the morning and was singing my son's nursery songs very loudly. The singing turned to screaming. My husband came into the room very quickly and got our son and then called my family to make arrangements to take me to the hospital. I started saying, "my life is going to be over, I'm in a trance and my world will flash by me." After about ten minutes I snapped out of the trance, but we knew I should go to the hospital.

We dropped our son off with my oldest sister so I could go to the hospital. This was a very sad day for me; I was crying so hard, worrying I would have to leave my newborn baby. I was breastfeeding, so my sister would have to give him formula while I was at the hospital. I thought I might be admitted again and not be able to leave the hospital. When I got to the hospital I met with a psychiatrist and I kept saying, "left brain, left brain, stay in the present." He prescribed me the same medication I was on in 2015 and then sent me home. I decided not to take the medication and focused on getting sleep and self-care. My family helped out a lot and I eventually was able to get some sleep and work past the feelings I was having.

Psychosis is something that can happen to new moms and I'm sure it's due to sleep deprivation and hormones. Also, having had gone through psychosis before, my chances were increased. Plus, it was winter, the time of year when I experience anxiety the most. I realized really quickly that I no longer wanted four kids, and I might only want one.

PICKING UP THE BROKEN PIECES

Every day as a new mom was a struggle. I could not get my son to nap for more than twenty minutes. I was exhausted and felt as if I didn't have any mother instincts. I would cry most days, feeling so inadequate. I tried everything to get my son to sleep. No one really tells you how hard it is to be a parent and how difficult the newborn stage is. You just don't have a clue until you're actually a parent.

One day I went for a walk with my two sisters and my sister-in-law. They started talking about how important sleep was, and it made me feel horrible. I yelled at them and said, "shut the fuck up about sleep, I have literally tried everything and my son just won't have long naps." I was so upset I walked quickly back to my car and told them I was leaving. My older sister who didn't have kids yet hopped in and I cried and talked to her on the way home about how much I was struggling. Being a new parent is not easy, and I feel that a lot of people don't talk about the mom guilt and the struggles that are involved in being a parent.

My son had colic and had a ton of stomach issues. He would go two weeks without pooping and would have the smelliest farts. When he was four months old, we were recommended by a doctor to starting feeding him foods such as prunes and avocadoes. This made a huge difference, and I finally started to feel stronger as a mother. I decided that I would no longer listen to what others had to say about napping, and I would truly become the mother I always wanted to be. His naps didn't really improve, but I no longer worked as hard at them because I felt that if he was not going to nap, I couldn't force him. I had read an article stating that babies are not robots and therefore you have to realize not all babies are the same. This helped me a lot, as I realized my son was different then the babies who napped easily and longer. I started to really enjoy being home with my son and ignored other mothers' opinions.

When my son was almost ten months old, I secured a home day care. I was so sad that I might miss him starting to walk on his own. I had gotten a job as a recruiter for a small company. I didn't feel as though I really fit in at the job, because I was older than the two girls I worked with and had a child. I was recruiting for sales, and my personality just did not match with this type of recruitment job. One day, I was asked to meet with my boss and she told me that they could no longer keep me on board due to financial reasons. I was so happy I couldn't wait to get my son and go home. Unfortunately, I had not worked long enough to collect unemployment insurance. A week after I had been let go from my job, there was a guy that looked at my LinkedIn profile. This guy had put down that he was working at the company I was let go from and it was basically the same job I had been doing. I felt so upset as I realized that my boss had lied to me. I emailed her, asking what was going on, and she responded that she did not need to give me a reason why she let me go and she was trying to be nice. This broke my heart even though I knew that I did not fit well with that job. I did, however, feel that I had contributed to the company and worked hard while I was there. I had so much anxiety not knowing why I was actually let go and it made me nervous to find another job in the wintertime. My self-confidence went down and I just felt so hurt.

I took a bit of time to enjoy with my son, but knew I needed to find a new job quickly. I was still paying for day care. In order to keep the day care secured, I had to keep paying or I would lose my spot. I called the placement agency I had used before, and there was an opportunity available. I was placed in a job as a benefits administrator. I had never done this type of job before other than setting up benefits for a few employees at the medical center. The person I was replacing was only going to be able to train me for three days. The job was hard and there was such a backlog of work that I felt overwhelmed. I was working with two benefits providers and had to do reconciliations, and I had no idea what I was doing. I told the agency that I would stay for two more weeks, but that the job was too much for me. This was only a three-month contract and I really should not have worried so much, but I put a ton of pressure on myself and wanted to do a good job. I was proud of myself that I stood up for myself and told the agency the job was causing me anxiety. I also let my boss at the new job know that I had been through some mental illness. My boss guilt-tripped me and convinced me to stay at the job. I of course told her I would stay the three months, even though in my heart I did not want to. I am such a people pleaser that I tend to alter my own opinion and values to please others. A few days later, I had about fifty phone calls and was trying to complete a hard task I had never done before. My heart started pounding in my chest and I felt hot. I told my colleagues I had a doctor's appointment I needed to go to as my boss was only in the office once a week. I packed up all my stuff and headed to my car. I got into my car and started screaming and shaking. I was having a panic attack. I called my husband and he came to pick me up. I then called the agency to let them know what had happened and that I would not be back at that job. I had to leave a voicemail as the person I dealt with did not answer the phone. I did not hear back from the agency until about a week later. Needless to say, they never called me back for any other jobs.

The day after I had my panic attack, I knew there was something wrong with me. Every winter I had so much anxiety that I did a lot of pacing around the room and wouldn't be able to sleep. I brought my son to day care and just tried to make it through the day. I felt this overwhelming sadness and fear all of a sudden. I called my sister-in-law and told her I felt that I might be bipolar. I cried and told her I just didn't know what I should do. She and her daughter came over for a visit to comfort and talk to me. I felt terrible not telling the rest of my family how I felt, but I didn't want to spark worry, so I asked her to keep it between us. My sister-in-law was very helpful and understanding and she said she thought it would be worth it to be assessed for bipolar if that's what I felt I may have.

I decided at this point I would seek out a psychotherapist and pay for it, as my husband's benefits would not cover it. I found that it helped having someone to talk to that was outside of my family. My psychotherapist definitely helps when I am being irrational, overthinking, and stressing over silly things. My psychotherapist suggested I make an appointment with my most recent psychiatrist and see if they would do an assessment. I went to the psychiatrist and explained the panic attack I had. He asked if I wanted to go on medication. I let him know I didn't want to go on medication because I hadn't needed medication after the short psychotic episode I had when my son was born. The psychiatrist looked at me and said, "if you don't want medication, why are you here?" I was so baffled. I was hoping he would give me advice on what I should do, but instead he basically said don't come here unless you want a prescription. I told him my psychotherapist suggested I make an appointment and look into having an assessment done. He responded that I had had one already and why would I do one again. I felt uncomfortable and I didn't want to talk to him about how I was feeling. I was so confused. I left the office and did not make a follow-up appointment. I decided I would keep seeing my psychotherapist instead, as she had compassion and actually cared about me as a human being. Over time I started to feel good again, and felt silly for thinking I may be bipolar and telling my sister-in-law.

After Christmas, I secured a permanent job as a bookkeeper. The owner of the company was great, and I really liked the job. It was a welcoming, family-oriented company, and I felt at ease . In January 2019, a permanent job opening came up at the place I had worked prior to going on maternity leave. My old colleague told me she was giving her two weeks' notice and she would recommend me for the job. I did not hear back from the company for a month. I assumed at this point I was not going to get an interview and I had no expectations that I would get to return to my previous job. I settled in at the new job and I started to get comfortable with my manager and co-workers. At the end of February, I received a call from my old company, inviting me for an interview. I was so excited and nervous. I had to call in sick and make excuses while interviewing. As I had said before, I hate lying and it gave me so much anxiety. After three interviews, I was finally offered the job. I was torn because I really wanted to go back to my old company where I loved the job, but I felt guilty quitting my current job. I kept going to psychotherapy to help with the decision-making process, and we agreed that taking the permanent job at my old company would offer more perks and I would receive great benefit coverage. This benefit coverage would also allow me to go to therapy more often and help my family through financial struggles. I mustered up a lot of courage and told my current employer that I had been given an amazing opportunity at my old job and I was giving my two weeks' notice. I felt horrible when my boss teared up, but they understood that they could not match the job pay or benefits. My boss wrote me a nice card and gave me a Tim Hortons gift card. I felt special, but terrible that I was leaving them even though I was really enjoyed working there.

CHAPTER 7

Christmas Stress

It is December 2019, and yet again as winter comes, my anxiety does too. I am sitting here, writing the final chapter of what my life is like now and what I can conclude from my experience. I am supposed to be hosting Christmas this year, and am currently six months pregnant with our second child.

My work got stressful, because everyone was trying to get everything done before the holidays. We work for a large company and there is a ton of paperwork to complete daily. I was getting about fifteen emails every hour, and am trying to train a new employee. The new employee is a wonderful person, but is also struggling with some personal issues. Her work has been affected and she has been making lots of errors. When the new employee makes errors, my other colleague and I have had to try and fix them while keeping up our busy daily activities.

I got an upper respiratory tract Infection and was feeling a ton a of stress. Last week the new employee made another mistake, and I just about had enough. The anxiety hit, I got hot, started to shake, and was staring at my computer blankly.

I realized I needed to go home. Before I left, I was able to cool down and not show any indication of how I felt. I told my boss I was not feeling well and had to leave for the day. I was coughing a lot, so it was obvious I was not feeling well. Leaving work was so much easier this time because I had no fear of being judged since I'm pregnant. I wish that leaving work because of anxiety is as easy as it was to say I'm pregnant or sick.

A few days before Christmas, my son got really sick with a high fever and was very lethargic. We gave him Tylenol for the fever and set timers in the night to check and make sure that his fever was monitored. I did not get a good night's sleep for a few days leading up to Christmas, and I was tired. He was also waking up every half hour, screaming. During the day, he would feel a bit better. On Christmas Eve we ordered in Chinese food and had my in-laws over as well as my husband's grandparents, who travelled a far distance and were staying in a hotel. My son was not feeling well and just before we ate dinner he threw up all over me right in front of my husband's grandma. I felt so awful for my son as I could tell he was embarrassed. We cleaned up and I gave my son a bath and then showered while my husband put pajamas on him. My son wanted to go straight to bed even though it was only 5:00. I was a bit sad as I was looking forward to putting out cookies and milk for Santa and carrots for the reindeer with him. I was also going to start the tradition of reading "'Twas the night before Christmas" and *The Grinch*. When I was a child, we always read "'Twas the night before Christmas" on Christmas Eve. When my husband was a child, they always read *The Grinch*.

Christmas Day came, and I was a bit of a mess. I was tired, but I wanted to make the perfect turkey dinner. I was so stressed about making the perfect stuffing that my mom usually makes at Christmas time. I took photos of the chopped celery to make sure it was the right size and I called her with a million questions. My in-laws were there to help too, but I explained I really wanted to make the stuffing just like my mom's. There were many other stressors that occurred in the day as well that I will not go into detail about. We planned on having the turkey dinner between 4:30 and 5:00 p.m. We checked the turkey at around 3:00 p.m. and to our surprise it was done. Luckily my in-laws were so helpful and said it would be fine, we would take the turkey out of the oven, cover it, and then put all the side dishes into the oven. Dinner did turn out delicious and was all ready for 4:30. After everyone had eaten, except my son who would not eat, I noticed that my son felt extremely hot. He said he wanted to go to bed. We checked his temperature and realized it was at about 103 degrees. We gave him Tylenol, put a cold cloth on him, and kissed him goodnight. As before, we set timers. We ate dessert then said goodbye to all our guests, except my in-laws, who were staying over. At about 8:30 p.m. we checked our son's temperature and the fever still had not broken. We decided it was time to take him to the hospital. We signed in to emergency and my son was given Tylenol as he had a fever. We were sent to emergency care and were hoping he would be seen quickly by a doctor. We waited at the hospital for about four hours. In the waiting room, my son puked on himself and my husband. We had packed some outfit changes, so it was okay. We finally got a room where he was given some Pedialyte and his temperature was checked again. The fever had finally broken, and when the doctor came, they said he had some sort of virus, and that we just needed to keep doing what we were doing already. His chest was clear and he was breathing okay, so we were sent home.

CHAPTER 8

Déjà Vu

On Boxing Day, I felt so relieved that Christmas was over. My son was still sick and had a two-hour nap, which was really nice. During his nap, I had a bath and just enjoyed the fact that the Christmas stress was over. At night, I felt anxious all of a sudden and was unable to sleep. I started having racing thoughts and I had the urge to try to write about how I was feeling. I told my husband I just needed fifteen minutes and I would be back to bed. I wrote on a piece of paper that "anxiety is an inner struggle that is hard to explain. I try to be strong and ignore it but it does not work. I become a total bitch when I am stressed and it is not until I hit my breaking point that I can talk about it. I struggle inside without knowing it myself until I break down."

After I wrote this, I froze for about a minute. I put my hands over my face and felt like the world had stopped and I was in the pitch dark even though the lights were on. I started to cry quietly to not wake my son or husband. I decided to go lie on the couch and try to fall asleep. I didn't want my husband to see me crying. I lay on the couch silently, with tears streaming down my face. I just kept thinking, *why does this keep happening to me*. My husband came downstairs at about the fifteen-minute mark to make sure I was okay. He gave me a big hug and said, "let's go to bed and we'll talk a bit." I tried different white noises to help me fall asleep. Eventually I fell asleep to the sounds of waves, which sounded more like a campfire and it brought back fond memories of camping with my family.

Morning came and I decided I wanted to find a psychologist to see if I had post-traumatic stress disorder or possible bipolar. I messaged with my brother-in-law, as typically I talk to him and my sister-in-law about my issues. They both go to therapy when needed and they always seem to say the right thing to make me feel better. I really appreciated that he understood and was even mentioning things I could do to help with the anxiety. He also told me about some good white noise apps.

I journalled a bit of what was going on. I wrote that there were multiple stages leading up to a stressful event such as a wedding or Christmas. "Stage 1: I try to do too many things at once and do only parts of the tasks. Stage 2: I become bossy/bitchy. Stage 3: The stressful event occurs and I soar through it but don't feel present. At Christmas, I felt like I was a robot on autopilot. Stage 4: Huge sense of relief, full of energy. Stage 5: I crash and feel like the world has stopped. Stage 6: Insomnia. Stage 7: I reach out and talk to so many different people and old friends. While going through anxiety I also tend to lose things and have a very bad short-term memory."

Throughout the day, I progressively got worse. In the afternoon, I went into a trance-like state and was screaming and saying, "it's happening again, no, no, no, my world is going to end, help me please, help, stop the trance, I'm going to forget everything and my life will be over." I then nodded my head and banged my feet and snapped out of it. After the trance happened, my husband called my psychotherapist and she suggested that I go to the hospital and have the baby monitored to be on the safe side. She said it could be pregnancy hormones that are causing the psychotic state. He also called my brother-in-law, who came and picked up my son and brought him to my oldest sister's house so that we could go to the hospital.

I went to the pediatric floor of the hospital to have the baby monitored. We told the nurse I was experiencing signs of psychosis. I was told that I would have to check in with emerge first and then they would send someone down to monitor the baby. I was so upset I started crying. I was hoping that they would monitor the baby and have a psychiatrist come talk to me. I could barely stand and was so distraught that they gave me a wheelchair to go down to the ER. We got in pretty quickly with a clinical psychiatrist. I explained what was going on and that I didn't want to take any medication, as I had been able to push through the last time without it. After we met, we waited in the waiting room for about three hours. Dinner time had passed, and I was hungry. I asked for some food and I was given a ham sandwich. I ate the bread and I didn't want to eat the meat as I have been cautious about what I eat during my pregnancy. Eventually I saw the doctor. Our baby was monitored and then we went home because everything looked good. My parents had picked up my son from my sister's and he spent the night at their house.

The next day I went into a trance-like state again. My husband called my other sister to see if she could help. I started screaming, "Tammy I will find your child." At that point, my husband decided that he should call an ambulance and I should be taken to the hospital. I ran down the road screaming a childhood friend's name and that I would find one of my old boss's child. The paramedics got me into the ambulance and I begged them to take me to a different hospital. They were unable to go to a different hospital because I was getting hard to manage and the other hospital in the area did not have a psych ward. I got to the hospital and was strapped to a bed. I absolutely hated that. I was then put into a small room like before to calm down and be assessed. During this time, I thought that I had multiple personality disorder as I did in 2015. I kept pointing at the cameras, thinking my family and old friends were watching a video of me. I thought that I was going to be famous and that my family was not actually my family. I believed that I was a genius and was going to save a child, and to do so I would have to die and come back to life. When I came back to life I would be with a new family and never see my family and old friends again. I thought all my friends and family were watching and crying, knowing that in order for me to save the child I would have to die.

I eventually was checked in on the floor for patients awaiting a bed in the psych ward. There was an old-school TV with VHS movies. I thought that I was from the past, and started arranging the movies based on everyone in my family. I thought that I was picking the movie each family member would like best and that would be their Christmas present. I acted as if I was the child from the movie *Home Alone*.

After being in the waiting room for some time, I was taken to Peekaboo. Peekaboo is a small floor with about six rooms. The first room I was in had a mattress on the floor and a metal toilet and sink. During this time, I did all sorts of strange things. I broke my glasses and twisted them, thinking I was cured and no longer needed glasses. I sang the song, "I Can See Clearly Now the Rain is Gone." I thought if I stuck my head in the toilet and blew bubbles it was the cure for cystic fibrosis. I then also drank the toilet water, thinking the cold water was the cure. My friend Amber's cousin died of cystic fibrosis and we had recently talked about him, so I'm assuming that is why it came into my head. Also, there are many ads that say "cystic fibrosis is like drowning on the inside."

During my first couple days in Peekaboo I was doing many missions in my head. I was still trying to find Tammy's daughter and to do so I would spin around the room and put my hands into a heart shape somewhere on the floor. I thought there was a camera and what I was doing was matching up to the map. I felt as though I was a CIA agent. Another vision I had was that I was helping my mother-in-law find her lost brother. My mother-in-law has not seen her brother in a very long time and he was living in a trailer somewhere in the forest. We had talked about him at Christmas and my oldest sister-in-law said this year she hadn't received a Christmas card from him. I had many more thoughts that came into my head, and they all seemed to relate to things I had talked about recently, or movies or TV shows I had watched.

I was given medication to help with the psychosis and within two days I started acting more like myself. I stopped hearing and seeing things that weren't actually there and I began to be more stable. The doctor wanted to keep me until the end of the week to monitor me with the medication. The medication is something that worked for me back in 2015, so it was good that it seemed to work quickly this time. My family visited me every day while I was in the hospital. I was so lucky to have my supportive family by my side; like last time, they helped keep me busy while I was in the hospital.

CHAPTER 9

My Journal

In this chapter I will provide the actual journal notes that I made each day while I was in the hospital for psychosis from December 29, 2019 to January 2, 2020. My intention is for you to see the real truth about my emotions, feelings, and sheer pain that I endured while being in the mental institution. I used writing in my journal as a coping mechanism, and found getting my thoughts down on paper relieved some of the anger I was feeling. This was a very difficult time for me, and I want my readers to understand what some mental hospitals are like. This is not written to deter anyone from going to a mental hospital, because as you can gather from what I was going through, this was the place that I needed to be. It is unfortunate that some mental health facilities do not have the funding that they truly require.

Dec 29, 2019

- Today I read the beautiful card my sister wrote for me. "Arielle, even though you are my little sister, you've taught me how to be a great mother, sister, and friend. You are stronger than you think and braver than you realize. This is just another bump in the road and like before you will get through this and come out even stronger. We are always here for you. Never be afraid to tell us how you feel and when you need to stop your job or whatever life throws at you. Let us know and we will be there for you. You are my best friend and I will always be there for you. Stay positive things with get better." This card made me feel so much better knowing my family is starting to get me. I hope my family will start understanding me a bit more and that when I stop working for example, they will understand that it's key, for I'm not doing well mentally. I have a very hard time sharing how I feel. I worry that I will be a burden or that I will worry my family. I can't wait to find out what is going on with me as it has been five years and every year around winter I have so much anxiety.

- I have been trying so hard to stay in the present and not think about the past.

- I remember all the things I was doing while in psychosis.

- I thought that my entire family were all imposters and that I was actually black and a singer.

- Another vision I had was that I was able to use all parts of my brain all of a sudden. This allowed me to see everything from my past and future. I felt that I was the most powerful and smartest woman in the world.

- I believed that my mom was the chosen one and my dad was God.

- I think I may have post-traumatic stress disorder, seasonal affective disorder, or bipolar.

- I had a vision that it was a long time ago and my brother came to a bar and was kicked out because his eyes were bloodshot. My brother has puffers and was not that drunk but was kicked out because the bouncers thought he was high. My brother's eyes were red from allergies. He told the bouncer that he needed his coat because it contained his puffers. I thought he was in a snowbank somewhere and I had to find him.

- During my psychosis, I was locked in a room and I thought I needed to break out. When the nurses came, I tried to sneak out, but they grabbed my arms really hard to stop me. I am twenty-nine weeks pregnant and they grabbed me so hard I actually have bruises on my arms. I understand now what I was doing in the room was harmful, but I'm sure there must have been a better way to stop me. My shoulder hurts, my arms, I am so sore.

- Our baby's heart rate was elevated when they last checked.

Dec 30, 2019

- There is no garbage can anywhere on this floor or anything to dry your hands on in the bathroom.

- I remember singing while in psychosis, "I don't give a fuck, I don't give a fuck." I think this is when I was a powerful woman and I was letting the world know that I have no shame.

- The toilet is metal which makes sense in the area I am in. The toilet is so cold and skinny it hurts to sit on it. I try to cover the toilet with toilet paper to make it less cold, but it keeps falling off. I literally feel like I am in prison. I haven't done anything wrong and I don't deserve to be here. I have some sort of mental illness, why am I treated as if I'm a criminal.

- The nurses and staff are really nice this time. I really want my book to do well so I can fix the mental ward and make it less like a prison.

- I am in Peekaboo, the worst possible place you could be! It's not much better than prison (Not that I have been there).

- Currently I am the only female in the room and it's scary. A guy said why are you here, you're too beautiful to be in a place like this. I told him I was having mental health issues. He said he has schizophrenia.

- The shower lock is broken so I had to have a nurse lock me in so no one could come in while I was showering. Once I was done, I would have to pull the emergency cord so they could come let me out. I was so scared they would forget about me.

- Today I am calm and completely feeling normal. Just feeling confused by what happened to me and why I did what I did. Jocelyn kept coming into my head and other childhood friends that I no longer talk to.

- The medication seemed to kick in fast, likely because I have used it before.

- I just found out I'm not allowed to have pencils, pens, or pencil crayons in this area. I won't be able to colour anymore. The nurse was so nice; she got me a few markers.

Dec 31, 2019

- Waiting for the doctor to come. I am so bored.
- You have to have staff to ring in phone calls for you. I hate having to keep asking for things.
- Staff is great and helpful, but I am going to go crazy if I have to stay in here much longer. I feel like I am in prison.
- I don't know when I will get a visitor, but hopefully soon.
- I am hoping to go home today. It's so uncomfortable here and I really miss my son.
- I just met with my doctor and they want to keep me three more nights. They believe it's possible that I am bipolar. The news of having to stay longer gave me so much anxiety that I threw up.
- Is seasonal bipolar a thing?
- I went into the washroom today and there was pee all over the seat and floor. I can't do this anymore. This place is awful. I was let into the other wing to use the washroom. The washroom toilet was covered in hair.
- Tomorrow is New Year's so I won't see my doctor. I will be stuck here.
- I don't think I can stay here that long. This place is a prison and horrible.

- My husband ordered baby monitors, a car seat, and a stroller.
- We were both afraid if the baby was okay, he was not going to order what we need in fear we may lose the baby.

Jan 1, 2020

- The shower here reminds me of camping. There are three sharp sprays that come out and you get cold because there's not enough water coming out. The towels are also really small and hard to dry your body with.
- Bring your own pillow if staying in the hospital as they are not comfy.
- Breakfast was just what I needed. All-Bran cereal, OJ, banana, cheese, coffee, and a muffin.
- Baby is kicking.
- Yesterday (New Year's Eve) I went to bed at 9 p.m. My mom called, but I told the nurse I was too tired to talk. The medication makes me so tired.
- I was going to call my mom back but there is a patient sitting where the phone is.
- The phone is in this small room with a TV and two tables that have four chairs attached.
- The patient was there yesterday when I tried to use the phone. The nurse told me to ask him to move to the other table and he said sure. In the process, he dropped his apple

sauce and it was all over the floor. Then he began moving and spilled his coffee on the floor too.

- This morning I wanted to call my mom, but the same patient was sitting by the phone so I am going to wait. The phone cord is really small so it's hard to talk and very uncomfortable.

- I'm showered, ate breakfast, talked on the phone. Now just waiting for my husband to arrive.

- I am bored as fuck!

- It's like time doesn't move!

- I'm sure it's very close to prison but there are more people in prison.

- The café is just like what you see on the show (*Orange Is the New Black*).

- Still waiting for my husband, I want to sleep, but I'm not sure when he is coming and don't want to be drowsy.

- I'm bored out of my fucking mind. I'm done with reading, I'm happy to write, but since I can only use markers in my area it's hard to write and so messy.

- There are two cameras in my room, as the staff watches all patients to ensure they are safe. I feel so self-conscious and awkward knowing they're watching me.

- I was just eating a muffin and it crumbled all over me and all I'm thinking about is, are they watching me?

- I also feel weird knowing that when I was psychotic, they saw it all. I was naked some of the times.

- The hospital air is so dry my nose has been bloody the whole time.

- I had a good visit with my son, husband, and father-in law. I feel so drowsy from the meds and my mood is a bit low. As much as I loved seeing them, I also was longing for a nap. It's too loud at this moment to nap and I can't stop coughing.

- I had a good nap and feel much better. My parents, siblings, sister-in-law, and my brother's girlfriend all came to visit. I am so lucky to have such a great, supportive family. My sister and brother-in-law brought pizza, wings, and garlic bread for lunch.

- I talked to a guy today that said when he gets discharged from the hospital, he has no home to go to.

- Right now, I am on a form three which means I'm involuntary and cannot leave without the doctor's approval.

- I am missing my house, husband, and son so much. I really want to go home tomorrow.

- I am also longing to go outside for some fresh air. I haven't been outside in days. I feel imprisoned and punished for having a mood disorder. This place is so depressing.

- There is a window in my room but the bottom part is tinted so you cannot see out the window unless you stand on something. (I'm only 5"1.)

- All the patients stare at my belly. One guy said, "hey pregnant, how are you?" I was a bit afraid he was coming closer to me and may try to touch my belly. Another girl said it was hard for her to look at me because she wants to be pregnant too. I said "I'm sorry to hear that. Do you have a husband or boyfriend?" She responded no, but she would find someone to do it. She has someone already willing. She also said she been a veteran for seven years and has so much intel on all the doctors in the hospital and was fighting against the queen.

- I went to use the washroom and again there was urine all over the seat and floor.

- I went to the washroom on the other side.

- I hope I get out tomorrow. (I didn't have to stay in Peekaboo anymore. I could go to south wing and share a room, but I had my own room and it was much quieter in the night.)

Jan 2, 2020

- Today is Thursday. My doctor said he would aim for me to go home on Friday. I am really hoping he decides to let me out today.

- I woke up a few times in the night. When I awoke it was 6 a.m. I went to the washroom, but there was urine all over the seat and floor. I went back to bed to sleep a bit more so I could ask to go to the other side where the toilets are not metal.

- It's 7 a.m. and breakfast won't come for another hour or so. I at least have some snacks and I'm sure if I asked, they would get me something. The nurses are all nice.

- Turns out breakfast is at 7:30 a.m. so I can eat and shower and get dressed before the doctor comes.

- I don't really want to shower as the shower is the worst, maybe I'll hold off and see if I get to go home.

- Being in here sure makes you realize the simple luxuries that you have at home. Such as a shower, a comfy bed, a fridge with food in it, the ability to eat what and when you want. I'm hoping my journal will be an eye opener for those who aren't taking care of themselves and could end up in a similar place as me. I also hope this book will raise awareness and help raise money to make mental health facilities better.

- I just ate breakfast and walked to take the tray to nurses. On my way, I walked past the washroom and there was a new guy going pee with the door wide open. I NEED to get out of here. Maybe I will transfer to the other area where I will share a room with a female at least.

- I don't feel safe here. I told the nurse an hour ago about the urine on the floor and it's still not clean. I want to get changed, but don't want to in my room because of the cameras.

- I think I'll shower so that I can get dressed and feel a bit cleaner.

- I met with my doctor and he is going to discharge me as long as my husband comes to pick me up. The doctor tried calling him while we were in a meeting room, but he did not answer. I tried after the meeting and he still did not answer so I tried calling my mom. I am feeling so angry.

I better get to leave today. I am trying so hard to remain calm, maybe this a test. I am just going to sit calmly until he calls back and I get to go home.

- Turns out it wasn't a test and when I went over to the south side of the ward my husband was waiting.
- We went upstairs where the café is for an hour so the nurses could complete the discharge paperwork. My parents met us there as well.
- I was so happy to get home, but I felt a bit on edge and weird. I took a shower and put all my clothes in the laundry basket.

That concludes my hospital journal. Next, I include some personal pieces from my continued journal. This was during a time I was adjusting to the lower dose of medication, and trying to cope. I am including this because I want my readers to understand that mental illness is no joke. A mood change can happen very fast. Writing can be a very powerful tool, and you may or may not choose to share. My husband did not know I was feeling this awful until he read what I shared with him. It was not easy to share my journal; I was really embarrassed, but I wanted him to have a good understanding of how I was feeling mentally. I understand that my entire family had to go through my experience with me, but I want them to know that it's not the same as living it. I want them to know that although I am home and no longer going through psychosis, this does not mean that I am cured. Most of my family does not know how I am daily. Mainly this is because I don't share. I hate it when people worry about me, and I have a hard time conveying what I am going through. My family sees me mostly in a good mood so me being bipolar didn't quite make sense to my parents. I don't talk about my manic episodes or the deep thoughts that I go through. The journal writing I am sharing here is from days when the reality that I am bipolar hit me hard.

Jan 26, 2020

- Today we got some stuff for the new baby and I am feeling a bit anxious.

- I felt so anxious during lunch today I couldn't sit still.

- The weather is so gloomy I just have this constant feeling of wanting to do something fun, but I don't have much energy. I hate winter so much.

- Every winter I wish I was on a tropical island.

- So excited to get the synopsis for my book. I really hope it does well so I can help a lot of people and hopefully pay off some of our debt so we can eventually afford to buy a house.

- The thought of spring makes me happy, but there's still so much time to go.

- I'm so sick of being pregnant, so glad this will be our last baby.

- I miss all the great things you can do when you're not pregnant. My husband is currently having a beer, it looks so good right now. I'm drinking milk, how exciting.

- I can't wait to have a sense of self again and not be a fat tubagoo.

- We just got back from a walk this afternoon. We had a great conversation about getting a nanny for our second child when I go back to work. This will take some stress off me as I would have to do double drop-off and pickup since my son will be going to school when my maternity leave is over. (My husband drives a work truck so I do all drop-offs and pickups.) I don't want to lose my job as it makes me so happy and I deserve to have a career too.

- Right now my son and husband are making a snowman in the backyard while I get dinner started.

- My thoughts never stop. I felt like screaming and punching something.

- It's so hard being me and I can't explain how I feel. I think when I go into a trance-like state and scream it's because that's my body's way of expressing how frustrated I am. It's blatantly obvious that I am bipolar. I have a ton of self-control, which is good. If I didn't, I think I would turn to self-harm. You just want to feel something and get your point across that things aren't great and I'm super frustrated. I fucking hate winter.

- My husband likes winter and is okay with relaxing during the day.

- I can't just sit down and chill because my thoughts don't stop! I think into the future and stress.

- Being pregnant doesn't help. I just want to run or do something but I can't. I feel imprisoned in my own thoughts. How do I make them stop?

- The word "fuck" feels so powerful. I think when I went through psychosis the reason why I kept saying fuck, fuck, fuckity, fuck is because it felt so good to say. When you have these intense thoughts, you keep them in your head because well it's not normal, it makes people worry.

- I'm not a person who cries much. Yes, I will during sad or really happy shows, but it's only tears and not really crying. When shit gets real, I can't really cry just tears and no sound. All I really want to do is scream to the top of my lungs and say FUCK ME THIS SHIT FUCKING SUCKS.

Jan 29, 2020

- Today I feel terrible. Every time I try to stand, I feel like I'm going to faint. I have no energy.

- I took an iron pill and ate more food, I am feeling a bit better.

- My son is crying saying he doesn't like day care and doesn't want to go. (My son goes to day care every Wednesday so I can focus on self-care.)

- I posted on Bell Let's Talk today. "I want to simply say: Do not judge someone until you have walked in their shoes and even then, you will never really understand how a person feels. We are all unique individuals and there is no one-size-fits-all with mental illness. Facial expressions don't always describe how the person feels inside. Be kind, be mindful, and don't make assumptions or judgements."

- I had a bath and relaxed a bit.

- It's hard being home alone all day because so many thoughts pop into my head.

- I had good thoughts, like my ambition to hold a charity event and raise money for the hospital I stayed in while going through mental illness. I want to purchase necessities such as toothbrushes, toothpaste, shampoo, conditioner, warm blankets, pillows, Kleenex, etc. The hospital has all these things, but they are not pleasant. I tried the toothbrush and every part of my mouth bled.

- The bad thought that came into my head today is that I could have killed our unborn baby during psychosis. I remember doing a somersault and grabbing my mattress and putting it up against the window and running into it to try and break out.

- Last week I told my mom to stop sending me videos of people who have mental health issues and have been through psychosis, but aren't bipolar. I felt that she was trying to say I'm being misdiagnosed. My mom usually calls me every day. She has not called me in a week and I think our conversation made her uncomfortable. She is still texting me, but it's clearly because she is afraid to talk and upset me. I know I need to give her time to come around, but I am freaking out.

- I just wish our family would go to therapy for me. I feel it's so good for everyone and I know it has helped me a lot. I also feel that if my son had a mental health condition, I would seek out therapy so I could learn how to help him. I feel so alone.

- I thought I was okay with my diagnosis, and I am in ways, but it's hard. My life feels like I will always have to worry about everything I do. I have to try to avoid stress so I don't go into psychosis. Medication should help, but the side effects are not fun. The medication I'm on currently makes me feel like a zombie.

- I know I'm not alone. I have people, but they talk about how hard it is to see me go through psychosis and then I just feel like a burden.

- If my son goes through something traumatic, I will check and see how he is doing every day and make him know he can talk to me about anything and that he would never be a burden. Although I will worry about him, I want him to be as open as possible and express himself however he feels fit. I express myself through writing.

- Everyone is so busy with their lives and I get it.

- I wish my family knew that although I'm not going through psychosis things are not okay in my head. Just because my actions are normal does not mean that my thoughts are good. I hate having to tell people. I guess I can't expect that from people, it's too much and not fair.

- People think with mental illness you can just be cured with medication, but you can't. There is so much more than just taking medication. Medication can't stop your thoughts.

CHAPTER 10

Family Members' Perspectives

Everyone in my family including my extended family has helped me in so many ways. I am very lucky that I have a family that was there for me and supported me throughout my entire illness. I cannot imagine how things would have been without their continued love and support.

This chapter was written by my sister and father. I am so fortunate to include something that they have written in my memoir, to give their perspective of how they felt during my mental illness.

Sister's Perspective

I never really fully understood the power mental illness has over one's mind and body until I saw someone so close to me go through it. When I first found out Arielle was in the hospital, I thought to myself: "don't worry, everything will be okay. I will go over there and talk to her and calm her down." I figured because I have such a close relationship with her I could make her feel better. I didn't realize the extent of what

I was walking into until I got there. When I opened the door, she was talking loudly and laughing hard to herself. She didn't even realize I was there. The words that were coming out of her mouth were something you would hear in a movie. It felt like she was playing a trick on us and that she was going to snap out of it at any moment. As the night went on, I quickly realized this wasn't the case. I remember the things she told me as she tried to work out what was wrong with her. She thought maybe she had been in a car accident and that she had killed us all. So many different scenarios played in her head. At one point she thought that she had been raped. These words made me sick to my stomach in fear that maybe it was true. Maybe something truly did happen to her, and this would explain why she was going through this. Maybe it was her brain's way of coping with the trauma. Once she was in a better state, she confirmed that it wasn't true and that it was her mind trying to come up with reasons to explain why this was happening to her. Throughout her journey, she had many thoughts, some more absurd than others. I distinctly remember her going up to a stranger and asking him if he was her father.

She had no concept of what was real. This made it a lot harder for the hospital staff to figure out what was wrong with her. Most doctors assumed it was drugs. It took a lot of time and advocating for her to get the tests she needed to rule out anything medical. Once they realized it wasn't medical, they started looking into mental illness, and they came to the conclusion that she was experiencing acute psychosis. Learning about what psychosis is helped us have a better understanding of what she was going through; however, it did not prepare us for the long road ahead to recovery.

Her being in the hospital was a real struggle for me. Even though she is my younger sister, I have always looked up to her. Anytime I had a problem she would always be there to comfort me and help me through it. She is my best friend and I felt like I was losing her. The one person I wanted to talk to everything about the most I couldn't. I wanted to be strong for her, but it started to become very hard as it was emotionally draining. We would often leave the hospital feeling so hopeful and then something would happen and we would be back to square one. I remember often crying myself to sleep. I just wanted everything to be back to normal. Every few days, we would go and visit her in the hospital. Playing cards helped normalize the situation as games are something that we would often play together. We started to notice small changes in her behaviour that felt positive; however, we did not want to get our hopes up. Once she had been released from the hospital for a long time, every time I received a call from my parents I worried that something was wrong. When I think back about my sister's journey through psychosis, I think about how hard it must have been for her. She lost many things that were important to her. She lost her job which she worked so hard at every day for two years. She lost the feeling of happiness due to the medication she was on, which meant she didn't fully enjoy her wedding day, something she had dreamed of since she was a little girl. She also lost her strength and will to live, which made us fearful every day as we were scared for her life. Throughout all of this, the one thing my sister didn't lose was her strength and courage. She was able to push through everything, which is not easy to do.

My sister said one of the hardest things is remembering everything she did and said while experiencing psychosis, so the fact that she has been able to share her story with the world in the hope to help break the stigma of mental illness is something I really admire. Having her go through psychosis more than once, my family and I can't help but feel a little uneasy sometimes. I want to believe that she's all better, but like with anything, things take time. She has worked hard toward making some changes in her life to better cope with her anxiety. This includes practicing self-care and seeing a therapist. She is also currently on medication that is being monitored, which has been a huge relief as we can see that it is working and is what she needs to feel more herself again. The things I have learned from her experience is to practice self-care and to never judge a book by its cover, because you never know what someone is battling. Mental illness is a horrible sickness that does not get enough attention from the media. We have come far from where we were; however, there are many changes that need to be made in order to help end the stigma.

Father's Perspective

It has been said, never judge a man until you have walked a mile in his shoes. A baby is born and we pray for its health, and when the baby has been deemed healthy, we are thankful. As we go through the life of the child, family becomes the most important part of a young life.

On January 12, 2015, we received a phone call from the hospital at 11:30 p.m., letting us know that our daughter was in a state of confusion. We immediately jumped out of bed and raced one hour to be by her side. Family is the most important thing there is. There is something about the bond between a mother and her child. My wife had that bond times ten over; she went to visit every day, with the promise of hope and a smile on her face despite the nights of crying herself to sleep. Over many months of visits to the mental health ward, mom was the rock. My wife and I have dedicated our lives to our four kids, and it has paid off as all three siblings came to the side of their sister in need. I know they will be by her side for as long as it takes, because when there is a strong family unit there is always hope.

CHAPTER 11
Understanding Mental Illness

Although my experiences were extremely terrible, I feel that I have become a much stronger person. I am not afraid to talk about what I went through or that certain situations make my anxiety worse. I am living a great life and know that life is not always perfect. Adult life is hard, and you have to take care of yourself. You are the person that controls your own destiny and therefore you must put in the hard work to feel better. I have learned to be an advocate for myself, and I tell people when they are stressing me out or I remove myself from the situation.

Physical impairments you can see. People with noticeable disabilities get help without even having to ask for it. People with mental illness have to be so strong, and they need to advocate for themselves. No wonder so many people with mental illness end up on the street or commit suicide. Never judge someone's actions, because you do not know what they are truly going though or why they may be doing what they are doing. As I mentioned in my chapter "Valentine's Hell," I ran through a hotel naked. I'm assuming most people who saw me thought I must have been wasted or on drugs. Since going through psychosis, I see the world completely differently, and I no longer judge the actions of others because I am not them and I do not know them, nor their situation.

I am lucky that I am an extrovert and have no fear in expressing myself. I can understand how difficult it must be for an introvert who does not share their feelings with the world and experiences a great deal of anxiety. This story is to help my readers know that you are not alone. I am usually outgoing and happy, but when I am not, no one knows because I can put on a persona that everything is okay even though it is not. My greatest struggle is communicating how I feel in a less aggressive approach. I tend to lash out or seem really frustrated when experiencing high stress and anxiety. Anxiety can be extremely hard to explain to those who do not suffer from it.

My husband came to a couple's psychotherapy session with me one time, and I feel we both learned a lot. I learned that I cannot control the emotions of others and therefore I should do my best to not think about people's reactions as much. For example, at Christmastime we received cards from family and friends. I had not gotten around to sending Christmas cards because I was struggling with anxiety. I felt more anxiety that I received these cards, but didn't send one in return. Our psychotherapist explained the whole purpose of them sending the card was just to say the person was thinking of us. Stressing out about it was doing the opposite of their nice gesture. The person who sent the card was not sending the card to get one in return. My husband asked the psychotherapist, "how can I react better to my wife's anxiety and help her rather than make her more upset?" The psychotherapist said to think of a situation with our son when he is scared to do something new, such as go down the stairs to the basement. You don't tell your son, "stop being afraid, you need to learn to go down the stairs by yourself." Instead you ask him, "why are you afraid to go down the stairs?" You sympathize with him and assist him to go down by explaining how to do it and that everything is okay and he does not need to be afraid. This was a great takeaway. I find that many times when I reach out and tell someone what I am going through they say I need to learn to relax and not stress myself out. To me this is hurtful, as part of the anxiety is that I cannot relax and when I can't sleep, I worry about the fact that I cannot sleep. Sympathizing with someone is much more effective than telling them they need to stop having anxiety or learn to cope. Most people who talk about their problems that aren't necessary and who have mental health issues are venting because they want you to sympathize with them.

Everyone in the world experiences anxiety, but I feel there are many different forms. I wish there was a different word for the intense anxiety. This anxiety is the one that is debilitating and may even cause you to miss work, school, family functions, or outings with friends. This anxiety could be you staring into space feeling confused and alone, overthinking, being terrified something awful may happen, running around doing many different tasks, throwing up, or having bad diarrhea. I have experienced every type of anxiety listed above and I'm sure I am missing many other types of anxiety people experience. I repeat a social interaction in my head over and over and worry that I may have offended someone or didn't say something I should have. I tend to overshare and talk a mile a minute when experiencing anxiety. I become overly extroverted and then go home worrying that I talked too much. Anxiety effects everyone in different ways. There are many people like me in the world, and no one would ever expect that I went through what I did unless I told them.

I hope that not only can I reach out to my readers, but that I can also raise some money to improve the system so no one has to feel like I did when I was in the mental hospital. I would like to donate money to assist those who don't have benefits and therefore cannot afford to go to therapy. Health care facilities should not be like a prison. The mental hospital should be a relaxing recovery place, not a nightmare. Anytime I have had to go back to this hospital or even go near it, I have a terrible feeling and I try not to think about the horrible experiences I have had there. Every year when winter hits, I feel post-traumatic stress and most is from what I went through, but part of it was the hospital.

It enrages me knowing that people are treated poorly for having mental health issues rather than being supported. I found out later how expensive it is to receive a diagnosis for a disorder, when in Canada health care is free. Psychotherapy is not covered in my husband's benefits, but yet he has coverage for basically everything else you can imagine. How is it that we live in a world where mental illness is not seen as a fundamental right to receive proper treatment.

I feel fortunate that my new company benefits covers the cost of all types of therapy, and therefore I am seeing my psychotherapist more frequently in the winter. Since my experience in 2015, I have always wanted to do something to help those who truly need it. I hope that by writing this novel

I can help others who have gone through what I have, or are on the brink of a mental breakdown themselves. Please learn from what I have gone through and know how important it is to find the right job for you and know when you need a break. There is nothing wrong with taking some time to yourself to feel mentally well. Speaking to someone outside of your friend and family group can really help.

Thank you for reading my memoir; I have enjoyed writing it. I hope that you now have a better understanding of mental illness and the importance of self-care. Please help me to end the stigma, and encourage others to read my memoir. I hope I can touch many lives and convey the importance of self-care and no judgment. I will use a large portion of my book sales to start initiatives for mental health that directly affect individuals. Mental illness should be seen the same way as with any medical illness. I am bipolar, but I will not let this define who I am! Being bipolar has pushed me to great extents and has made me into the strong and courageous woman that I am. I won't stop fighting to end this terrible stigma and help those who are in need.

You are not alone. Fight hard, because the world needs people like us.

APPENDIX

My Tips to Help a Person Struggling with Mental Illness

- Find out what triggers the person and do you best to avoid doing or talking about things that could cause distress and anxiety. This does not mean you have to walk on eggshells and be worried to say anything. Asking the person what bothers them can truly help.

- Reassure the person how much you love/like them and why, talk about their good qualities and give examples. For example, my psychiatrist talked about how one day I was in the waiting room eating a granola bar when another psychotherapist asked who the awesome pregnant girl was. She said, "that's Arielle and she's pretty chill." She said this during one of our sessions where I was being hard on myself and feeling that I talk too much sometimes. My psychotherapist pointed out that people obviously like me the way I am or they would stop talking to me. This made me feel much better as I do like that. I have a carefree attitude and can be myself in front of others.

- Simply be there to listen and **do not** try to fix their problems. Leave the fixing to the medical professionals.

Respond with answers such as "that sounds tough," or "is there anything I can to help?" Please refrain from telling the person they need to learn not to stress so much. This is not helpful, as I'm sure this is a known fact for the person experiencing mental health issues.

- If the person is having a rough day, remind them of things they can do that are therapeutic. Some examples could include, colouring, journalling, knitting, yoga, going for a walk, reading a good book, or watching a funny show that doesn't involve a lot of thinking.

- Mental illness is not a one-size-fits-all situation. Don't compare your friend or family member to someone else who has the same disorder.

Canadian Mental Health Association Tips for Supporting Someone You Love

https://cmhaww.ca/documents/depression-and-bipolar-disorder/

- Learn more about the illness and listen to your loved one so you have a better understanding of their experiences.

- Someone who experiences an episode of depression may want to spend time alone or act out in frustration, and this can hurt other people's feelings. These are just symptoms—it isn't about you.

- Ask your loved one how you can help. Think about practical help with day-to-day tasks, too.

- Make sure your expectations are realistic. Recovery takes time and effort. It means a lot when you recognize your loved one's work toward wellness, regardless of the outcome.

- Make your own boundaries, and talk about behaviour you aren't willing to deal with.

- Seek support for yourself and think about joining a support group for loved ones. If family members are affected by a loved one's illness, consider family counselling.

Suggestions of Things to Bring to a Mental Health Facility

- Cozy blanket
- Snacks you enjoy
- Peppermint tea
- Cards
- Card games (Wizard, Monopoly Deal, Uno)
- Warm socks
- Shampoo, conditioner, body wash
- Toothbrush and toothpaste
- Comfy clothes
- Pillow
- Kleenex

- Colouring books
- Markers
- Inspirational books
- Journal
- Magazines

Phone Apps

- What's Up
- Headspace
- Apple Podcasts
  (Jason Newland, "Let me bore you to sleep")

Website with Mental Health Resources in Canada

https://www.ctvnews.ca/health/mental-health-care-in-canada-where-to-find-help-1.3767445

(Bell Media, January 29,2020)

ACKNOWLEDGMENTS

I want to thank my parents for lending me the funds to self-publish my memoir. My parents would do absolutely anything in the world for me. I appreciate my mom coming to watch my son so I could make to it to all my psychiatrist and psychotherapy appointments. While I was in the hospital, my parents came every day, which I can understand is tough as they had to drive an hour there and home as well as witness their daughter so torn and upset about staying in the mental health hospital. Thank you for staying by my side every step of my mental health journey.

I want to acknowledge my husband who was my constant and remained with me throughout my psychosis, anxiety, and depression. My husband could have easily called off our engagement and run for the hills, but he didn't. He has been so supportive of me writing my memoir and has been willing to do what is needed for me to cope with my illness. I feel so lucky to have such an amazing, caring, supportive husband.

My sisters and brother have been so supportive of me writing my memoir, and everything that I have gone through. I feel so blessed coming from a big family, as I have such wonderful siblings. My sisters, their husbands, and my brother and his girlfriend visited me in the hospital and helped my mood incredibly. I have never felt so much love and compassion as when my family stepped up and did everything in their power to ensure that my days in the hospital were eventful, and that I knew they were there for me.

I also want to thank my extended family for being so caring toward me and always saying the right things that either made me laugh or made me feel better about my situation. My mother- and father-in-law came and visited me while I went through psychosis and depression. They made light of my situation and kept my mood up by showing me that I am a part of their family. My sisters-in-law and brothers-in-law made it clear to me that I always have someone to talk to and they have given me ideas on how to cope with my illness. My oldest sister-in-law and her children sent me adorable cards when I was going through psychosis in 2015, and it helped me to know that I was not alone and had so much love from our families.

I want to give a big thank to my psychotherapist who has gotten to know me so well and has changed my life immensely. She was the very first person who took me on as a patient right away without a wait and made sure that I was being properly cared for. She has helped me to understand when I am being irrational or hard on myself. She has also pushed me to care for myself more than I ever have in my life. I am grateful to have met someone who cares about me as a person and would go to great extents to ensure my well-being.

Lastly, I want to thank all the friends that I confided in and who responded to me in a positive and caring manner. My friends have all said they will purchase my book, and would love to celebrate my accomplishment.

CPSIA information can be obtained
at www.ICGtesting.com
Printed in the USA
BVHW081548050321
601818BV00002B/613